Welcome to Graceland

Graceland is a very special place for both of us. We have so many wonderful memories of the time we shared here with all our family and friends, and with a monumentally important person in our lives whom we shall always love, Elvis Presley. It would be impossible to tell you how much Graceland means to us, or how much it always meant to him. It will always seem like home.

Elvis was very proud of Graceland, and he often showed it off to friends and fans. You might even say he was the original tour guide. When we opened Graceland to the public in 1982, we felt certain that he, more than anyone, would have been so pleased that the whole world would have a chance to share the home he loved so much, and have the opportunity to learn more about his phenomenal life and career. Graceland is the ultimate tribute to this very special man.

We sincerely hope that this book, with all its stunning photography and fascinating information, will be a treasured keepsake of your visit to Graceland. Or, if you have not yet visited, we hope it will give you the feeling of being here until you can make the trip.

It is our pleasure to share Elvis Presley's Graceland with you. It was his own private corner of the world, a place where he felt comfortable, secure and happy. Elvis always made his special guests feel welcome and very much at home. We, along with all the management and staff of Graceland, hope you feel the same way.

Sincerely,

Priscilla Presley
Priscilla Beaulieu Presley

Lisa Marie Presley
Lisa Marie Presley

Dick Zimmerman / Shooting Star

Elvis Presley's Graceland

THE OFFICIAL GUIDEBOOK

Inside front cover photo: Graceland Mansion today.
Front Cover Flap: Elvis Presley in front of Graceland Mansion in 1960.
Opposite Page Top: 1971 family portrait of Elvis, Lisa Marie and Priscilla Presley.
Opposite Page Bottom: Recent portraits of Priscilla and Lisa Marie.
Above: 1958 portrait of Elvis and his parents, Vernon and Gladys, in Graceland's living room.

Above: The candlelight vigil is a moving and beautiful tribute to Elvis. Each year on August 15, the eve of the anniversary of his death, the gates of Graceland Mansion open shortly after 9:00 PM for anyone who wishes to walk up the driveway to Elvis' grave site and back, carrying a candle in quiet respect. The gates remain open until all who wish to participate have done so.
Right: The wrought iron entrance gates with a musical flourish were added by Elvis during his first year of residency at Graceland.
Center: On November 7, 1991, Graceland was honored with a listing in the National Register of Historic Places. This marker is in place on the front lawn of the estate.

Original Edition, © Copyright 1993
Revised Edition, © Copyright 1996
Graceland Division,
Elvis Presley Enterprises, Inc.
3734 Elvis Presley Boulevard
Post Office Box 16508
Memphis, Tennessee 38186-0508
(901) 332-3322 &
1-800-238-2000
Graceland is a division of Elvis Presley Enterprises, Inc., a corporate entity wholly owned and operated by the Elvis Presley Trust. Elvis, Elvis Presley, TCB, and Graceland are registered trademarks of Elvis Presley Enterprises, Inc. All rights reserved. This book, or parts thereof, may not be reproduced in any form without permission.

Produced by:
Legacy Communications, Inc.
4239 Grand Avenue
Ojai, CA 93023
Printed in Korea
2nd Printing, 1996

Writers: Laura Kath, Mariah Marketing, with Todd Morgan, Graceland.
Project Managers: Laura Kath and Tom Burkett. Graphic Designers: Peggy Ferris and Roger Morrison
ISBN 1-56933-018-2
Library of Congress 93-086633

Photo Credits and Acknowledgments

All photographs utilized in the publication are the © copyrighted material of Elvis Presley Enterprises, Inc., all rights reserved. Photographs may not be reproduced without permission.

Current location photography by Gil Michael and Pauline Cuevas, Gil Michael Photography of Memphis.

Historical Elvis Presley photography from the Graceland Archives.

Special thanks to:
Todd Morgan, Director of Creative Resources, Graceland, and supervisor of this book project.

Brett Guin, Graceland security staff member and general assistant/facilitator for the primary Graceland photo shoot.

Amy Silberberg, Graceland design staff member and project supervisor for the 1996 revisions.

Greg Howell, Liz Awsumb, Bettina Ong, and Angie Hadley, Graceland archival staff members, and facilitators for the 1996 revisions.

In appreciation: Delta Presley Biggs, Elvis' paternal aunt residing at Graceland from 1967 until her death, July 29, 1993.

Dedicated to the memory of Elvis Aaron Presley, 1935-1977

Above: Elvis greets two fans at the gates of Graceland in his 1956 Purple Cadillac circa 1957.
Below: The Alabama fieldstone fence and brick wall surrounding the gate guardhouse were added by Elvis shortly after his purchase of Graceland in 1957. Visitors from around the world have scribbled their messages and tributes on the wall ever since. The current guardhouse was added by Elvis in 1971, replacing the original wood structure.

Elvis at Graceland, home on leave from the army, 1958.

Contents

Part 1

Elvis' Early Years and Musical Beginnings

1935 – 57

Pages 8 – 13

Part 2

Elvis' Life at Graceland

1957 – 77

Pages 14 – 59

Part 3

Elvis' Legend Lives on at Graceland

1977 –

Pages 60 – 71

Left: The "Elvis Country" LP album cover features a photo of Elvis at age three.
Center: Elvis at Graceland, 1957.
Right: The Elvis Presley commemorative U.S. postage stamp first issued January 8, 1993.

Part 1

Elvis' Early Years and Musical Beginnings
1935 - 57

Opposite: This shot from a 1955 Florida performance is classic early Elvis. It was used on the cover of his first album, "Elvis Presley".
Bottom Left: The two room Tupelo, Mississippi house of Elvis' birth.
Bottom Right: Elvis' Humes High School diploma dated June 3, 1953.

*Elvis was named after his father, Vernon Elvis Presley, and Mr. Presley's good friend, Aaron Kennedy. "Aron" was the spelling the Presleys chose, apparently to make it similar to "Garon", the middle name of Elvis' twin. Toward the end of his life, Elvis sought to change the spelling of his middle name to the traditional and biblical "Aaron". In the process he learned that official state records had inexplicably listed it as "Aaron" anyway, and not "Aron" as on his original birth records. "Aaron" is the spelling his family chose for his tombstone, and it's the spelling his estate has designated as the "official" spelling when the middle name is used today.

In a two-room house in Tupelo, Mississippi at 4:35 AM on Thursday, January 8, 1935, Elvis Aaron* Presley was born, the second boy in a set of identical twins. The first, Jessie Garon, was stillborn. Elvis would be the only child of Gladys Love Smith Presley and Vernon Elvis Presley. The Presleys and their relatives were a close-knit, hardworking family that attended the First Assembly of God Church where young Elvis loved to sing gospel. He also grew up listening to the black blues men in the neighborhood and to country music on the radio.

Early on, Elvis displayed notable singing talent. In the fall of 1945, ten-year-old Elvis entered the youth talent contest at the Mississippi-Alabama Fair & Dairy Show held in Tupelo. He sang "Old Shep" and won the second place prize of $5.00 and free admission to all the fair's rides. Months later, Elvis received his first guitar, an inexpensive model purchased by his mother at the Tupelo Hardware Store. The Presley family lived in several different houses in Tupelo over the years, and Vernon and Gladys worked from job to job, trying to achieve a better standard of living. In late 1948, they packed all their belongings into a trunk and strapped it onto the on top of their car, and moved a couple of hours' drive north to Memphis, Tennessee, where they hoped opportunities would be greater.

Through much of Elvis' school years, he and his parents lived in public housing in the poor neighborhoods of north Memphis. Elvis attended Humes High School and worked odd jobs to help support his family. The teenage Elvis bought his clothes on Beale Street and absorbed the black rhythm & blues and gospel music he heard there. He also enjoyed attending all-night gospel sings downtown. He continued to sing and play guitar, wore his hair long (by that day's standards) and slick, with sideburns. During his senior year at Humes High, Elvis won the annual school talent show, performing "Keep Them Cold Icy Fingers off of Me" and receiving more applause than any other contestant.

After graduation on June 3, 1953, Elvis went to work at the Parker Machinists shop. That summer, Elvis nurtured his hopes of a singing career when he stopped by Sun Records producer Sam Phillips' Memphis Recording Service. Phillips wasn't in, but his assistant Marion Keisker helped Elvis cut a $4.00 demo acetate record of "My Happiness" and "That's When Your Heartaches Begin". Elvis reportedly gave this record to his mother as an extra, belated birthday present (her birthday was April 25). Elvis then began driving a delivery truck for Crown Electric Company and attended electrician's school at night.

In January 1954, Elvis reportedly made another $4.00 acetate record at Sun. This time producer Sam Phillips was in, and seemed mildly interested in Elvis' raw talent. That summer Phillips was looking for a singer to record "Without You", and Marion Keisker remembered Elvis and suggested to Sam Phillips that he give him chance at it. Elvis did not perform the tune to Phillips' satisfaction.

The Early Years 9

But, after Elvis teamed up with local musicians Scotty Moore on lead guitar and Bill Black on bass, everything clicked on July 5, 1954, when the guys broke into a sped-up version of Arthur Crudup's blues song "That's All Right". Phillips was so impressed that he immediately recorded it, and soon after recorded Elvis' up-tempo version of Bill Monroe's "Blue Moon of Kentucky" for the flip side of the record.

Phillips took acetates of Elvis' first commercial record around to local Memphis radio disc jockeys. WHBQ disc jockey Dewey Phillips (no relation to Sam) played "That's All Right" on the radio. The phone rang off the hook with listener requests to hear it again and again, prompting Dewey Phillips to bring Elvis in that night for a live interview, and making him an overnight celebrity in Memphis. Sam Phillips signed Elvis to his first recording contract with his own Sun Records label later that month. Elvis, along with Scotty and Bill, began touring and making personal appearances around the South, supporting his eventual five Sun singles, which were regional hits. Elvis' one appearance on the Grand Ole Opry that fall was met with a less than enthusiastic response, reportedly prompting talent coordinator Jim Denny to suggest that Elvis go back to driving a truck! But, Elvis soon garnered a long-term performing contract with the "Louisiana Hayride", a Saturday night country music radio show originating in Shreveport, Louisiana and broadcast over KWKH Radio, a direct competitor to Nashville's Grand Ole Opry radio program. During this time, drummer D.J. Fontana joined the band.

In the latter half of 1955, a promoter Elvis met during his appearances on "Louisiana Hayride" Colonel Tom Parker, became involved in Elvis' career, and soon became his official and exclusive manager. (Scotty Moore had been the manager early on, followed by Bob Neal, who continued to consult for a while after Colonel took over.) In the fall of 1955, Colonel Parker negotiated the sale of Elvis' Sun Records contract to RCA Records. Elvis was definitely the hottest new star in the music business.

Two days after his twenty-first birthday, Elvis had his first recording session for RCA in their Nashville studios on January 10, 1956. "Heartbreak Hotel" was cut that day and released on January 27. It soon hit number one on Billboard's pop singles chart, staying in the top spot for eight weeks and becoming Elvis' first million-selling (or gold) single. The song also crossed over to hit number one on the country chart and top five on the rhythm & blues chart. In March, RCA released his very first album. Titled "Elvis Presley", it soon found its way to Billboard's pop album chart for a long run, with ten weeks at number one.

Elvis' network television career was launched on January 28, 1956 with the first of his six appearances on the Jackie Gleason produced "Stage Show" variety program on CBS, hosted by Tommy and Jimmy Dorsey. On April 3, 1956, Elvis made the first of his two appearances on "The Milton Berle Show" on ABC. On the second show on June 5, he performed a sensuous gyrating version of "Hound Dog", causing much consternation amongst adult viewers and wild excitement among teenagers. On July 1, 1956, Elvis did a tamer version of "Hound Dog" sung directly to a Bassett Hound on "The Steve Allen Show" on NBC. Finally, Elvis was invited by television's most popular variety show host, Ed Sullivan, to make three appearances on his program for a total of $50,000, at that time by far the largest amount ever paid to a performer to appear on television. On September 9, the first of these three Sullivan appearances attracted 54 million viewers, then the largest television audience ever.

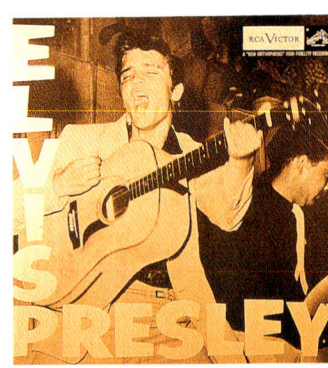

Above: "Heartbreak Hotel" was the first Elvis single to sell more than one million copies, thus becoming his first gold record. The award is displayed in his trophy building at Graceland.
Below: "Elvis Presley" was Elvis' first record album, also his first gold album.

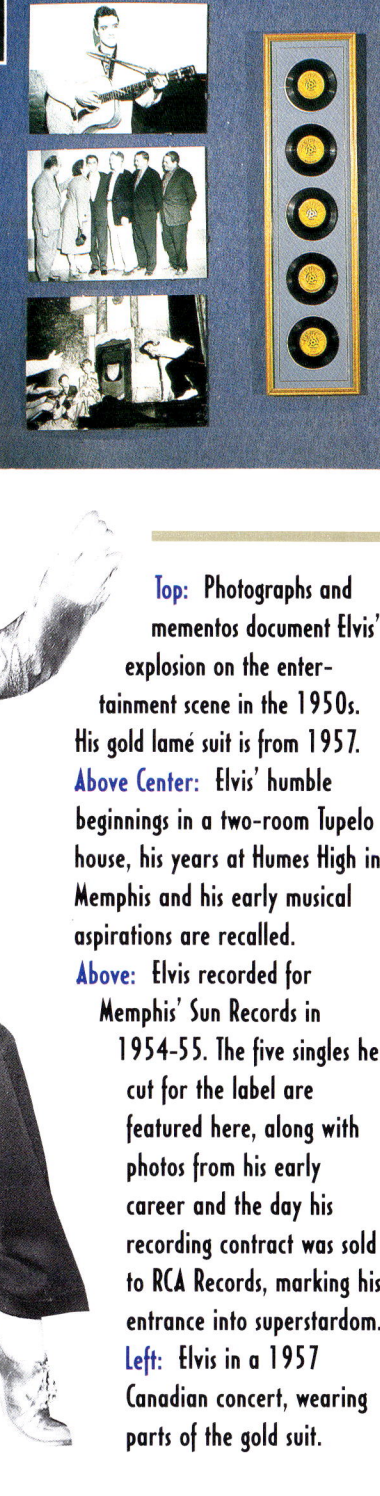

Motion pictures had already beckoned this intriguing new star. Elvis screen tested with Paramount in Hollywood in April 1956 and signed a seven-year movie contract. He shot his first movie in August on loan-out from Paramount to Twentieth Century Fox. Entitled "Love Me Tender", it premiered in November 1956 at the Paramount Theater in New York City and became a smash hit along with the title song.

Meanwhile, Elvis continued to perform and make personal appearances all around the United States. His audiences grew bigger and bigger, wilder and wilder, increasing his fame. Colonel Parker developed souvenir Elvis merchandise including t-shirts, hats, belts, purses, jewelry, stuffed hound dogs, even a cologne. Elvis fans created pandemonium wherever he appeared. On January 6, 1957, two days before his twenty-second birthday, Elvis made his third and final appearance on "The Ed Sullivan Show". This was the famous "waist-up" camera angle, censoring Elvis' controversial pelvic and leg gyrations. Ironically, Ed Sullivan himself helped to diffuse some of the controversy when he said on the air "this is a real decent, fine boy" and he had "never had a pleasanter experience on our show with a big name than we've had with you. You're thoroughly all right." High praise indeed for the boy from Memphis, pursuing his American dream with a unique musical blend of white country and pop, black rhythm & blues, and gospel, delivered with talent, credibility, and enormous charisma.

For Elvis, dubbed by the fans and media as the King of Rock & Roll, 1957 was another banner year. He continued touring and performing all over the United States, including Hawaii, plus five shows in three Canadian cities. That year he also filmed and released his second and third movies, "Loving You" and "Jailhouse Rock" with accompanying hit soundtrack recordings. In between career commitments, Elvis managed to return to Memphis long enough to purchase Graceland in March 1957.

Celebrating his first Christmas at Graceland that December, Elvis received his official draft notice from the United States Army. His induction was postponed just long enough for him to complete filming his fourth motion picture, "King Creole", considered to be his finest acting performance. His co-star Walter Matthau once said "He was an instinctive actor ...he was very intelligent ...he was not a punk. He was very elegant, sedate, and refined, and sophisticated." Elvis' star shone brightly over acting, singing, recording, and live performances. His next role, however, required only United States citizenship and "basic training".

Top: Photographs and mementos document Elvis' explosion on the entertainment scene in the 1950s. His gold lamé suit is from 1957.
Above Center: Elvis' humble beginnings in a two-room Tupelo house, his years at Humes High in Memphis and his early musical aspirations are recalled.
Above: Elvis recorded for Memphis' Sun Records in 1954-55. The five singles he cut for the label are featured here, along with photos from his early career and the day his recording contract was sold to RCA Records, marking his entrance into superstardom.
Left: Elvis in a 1957 Canadian concert, wearing parts of the gold suit.

The Early Years 11

Elvis' Army Years 1958 - 60

On March 14, 1958, Elvis was inducted into the United States Army at the Memphis Draft Board and assigned serial number 53310761. On March 25, at Fort Chaffee, Arkansas, he received his indoctrination exam and famous haircut, eliminating his long hair and sideburns. He was then assigned to basic training at Fort Hood, Texas. Private Presley was stationed there for six months and his parents joined him at a temporary home near the base.

In August 1958, Gladys Presley became ill and returned to Memphis to be hospitalized with acute hepatitis. Elvis was granted emergency leave and arrived in Memphis on the afternoon of August 12. Gladys Presley died in the early hours of August 14 at the age of 46. She lay in state at Graceland and services were held at the Memphis Funeral Home on August 15. Elvis was devastated by his mother's passing, but returned to his army duties on August 25.

Elvis left the U.S. for his eighteen-month assignment to West Germany in September 1958.

His father Vernon Presley and grandmother Minnie Mae Presley lived with him in his off-base residence in Bad Nauheim. It would be there, in late 1959, that Elvis would be introduced to Priscilla Ann Beaulieu, an American Air Force captain's daughter, who would later play a significant role in his life and legacy.

Elvis achieved the rank of private first class in November 1958, specialist fourth class in June 1959, and sergeant in January 1960. He was honorably discharged on March 5, 1960. Elvis received no special privileges as a famous soldier and worked doubly hard to prove that he was serving his country just like any other G.I.

Part of Elvis' personal commitment was that he did not perform in concert during his two years in service though he was often asked to do so. Although he worried intensely that so much time away from entertaining and movie-making might destroy his career, he needn't have been concerned. Elvis' greatest successes were yet to come.

Above Center: Elvis on maneuvers in West Germany, 1959.
Above Right: Memorabilia and mementos from Elvis' 1958-60 army career are displayed in this area of his Graceland trophy building.

Opposite Page
Center: For this special photograph, the Presley Estate's full inventory of Elvis' guitars is displayed on the staircase in the Graceland Mansion foyer. On any given day, visitors see many of the guitars in the various exhibits, while the rest usually remain in storage. An interesting component of this collection of stringed instruments is an old Stradivarius-copy violin that had been tucked away in one of Elvis' closets. He was actually known on rare occasion to strike a few chords on the fiddle in private, but not on stage.

Inset Left: Elvis poses with his Gibson Doubleneck for a movie publicity shot.
Below Left: Elvis in a scene from his second film, "Loving You" in 1957.
Below Center: The Burns of London Double Six was used in the movie "Spinout".

Below Right: During his 1969 Vegas engagement, Elvis performs with his personalized 1956 Gibson J-200, a longtime favorite.
Inset Right: Elvis with his "Chet Atkins Country Gentleman" edition Gretsch guitar, pauses to share a story with his Vegas audience, 1969.

Elvis Presley's Graceland

The Early Years **13**

Part 2

Elvis' Life at Graceland 1957 - 77

Opposite: Elvis' famous 1955 Pink Cadillac Fleetwood sedan, his mother Gladys' favorite automobile, and probably the most famous car in the world.
Right: The rooms on the first floor all boast the original molding, partially gilded for emphasis, as in the stair hall, lined with smoked-glass mirrored panels and topped with a Maria Theresa-design Italian cut glass chandelier (one of three purchased by Elvis in 1974 at Belvedere Lighting in Memphis).

Visiting Elvis Presley's Graceland in Memphis, Tennessee is not just another famous house or museum tour. Graceland is and will always be Elvis Presley's family home, a place full of the same joys, laughter, sorrow and tears experi-enced in your own home. When Elvis was a poor youngster, he frequently told his parents that some day he would make a lot of money, buy them the finest house in town, and end their years of hard work and financial struggle. On March 26, 1957, at the age of 22, Elvis made good on that promise with the purchase of Graceland Mansion for $100,000. The emerging king of rock & roll now had his castle. Over the years that Elvis lived here, and in the years since he died here, Graceland has come to mean so many different things to many different people. But most importantly, it still represents, just as it did for Elvis, a part of the American Dream.

Graceland began as a 500-acre farm owned by the S.C. Toof family. In 1939, a Southern colonial mansion was commissioned by Ruth Brown Moore and her husband Dr. Thomas Moore to be built on 13.8 acres of this land. Mrs. Moore's great-aunt was the Grace in "Graceland", the name of the original farm. The new house now took on the same name. In October 1940, a reporter from the *Memphis Commercial Appeal* wrote, "Located well back from Highway 51 in a grove of towering oaks, it stands proudly on land that has been in the family nearly a century. As you roll up the drive, you sense its fine heritage of the past in its general feeling of aristocratic kindliness and tranquility." The feeling is much the same today.

Many additions and changes were made to the mansion and grounds during Elvis' years at Graceland, including incorporation of trendy 50's, 60's and 70's era decor. Even though the estate was guarded and the house a refuge from the media and fans, Elvis loved showing people his home. There were never any organized tours like today, but Elvis' family and friends recall his always saying to others "Come to Memphis, I want to show you Graceland." Elvis is thus regarded as Graceland's original tour guide. Therefore, today's tour guides show over 700,000 visitors a year things that Elvis included on his standard tour. The second floor of the mansion containing Elvis' private bedroom, wardrobe room, bath, and office; Lisa Marie's bedroom and bath; and an additional bath and dressing room are not part of the tour.

Life at Graceland 15

The Living Room and Music Room

Right: The living room, with its 15-foot custom white sofa and gracious appointments was far more lived in than its formality suggests. This blue, gold, and white color scheme was typical of these rooms in the late sixties and early seventies. While Elvis changed the color scheme again and again through the years, the key furnishings were constant. The stained glass peacocks, designed by Laukhuff Stained Glass of Memphis were added during a redecorating done by Elvis in 1974, which included putting these original furnishings in storage in favor of a mostly red look. (The blue and white look was brought back when Graceland opened for tours in 1982, and the "red look" went into storage.) Beyond the peacocks is the music room where many a night Elvis and friends sang their favorite tunes. The living room measures a comfortable 17' x 24' and the music room is 14' x 17'.

Below: In the living room Elvis plays one of his guitars for a mid-sixties Memphis newspaper feature about the star at home.

Inset Left: The portrait of Vernon Presley in the living room was Vernon's Christmas gift to Elvis in 1976, Elvis' last Christmas.

Opposite Right: From 1974 on, this beautiful ebony Story & Clark baby grand piano graced the intimate music room. A white baby grand, which Elvis traded in on the purchase of this one, was the longtime favorite. For a brief time, a gold-leafed grand piano occupied this spot.

16   *Elvis Presley's Graceland*

The Dining Room

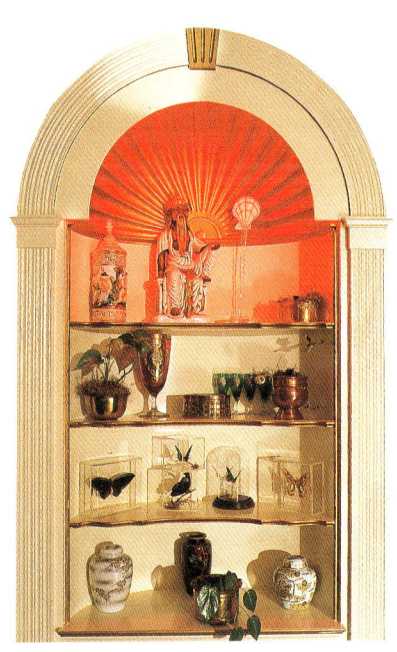

Left: Across the foyer from the living room is the dining room where Elvis and his ever present entourage of family, friends, and personal staff would crowd around the eight-foot table. Here they would enjoy great Southern cooking, play a little low-to-no stakes poker, and swap stories. The main Christmas tree was placed in the dining room each holiday season, often in front of the large north window, with the adults exchanging gifts on Christmas Eve and Lisa Marie waiting until Christmas morning. The approximate dining room dimensions are 17' x 24', with a nine-foot ceiling.
Above: Corner shelf units, accented by reddish neon, contain original pieces of artwork and bric-a-brac enjoyed by Elvis and his family.

Inset Left: This photograph was taken from Elvis' perspective sitting at the head of the dining table. Evening meals were typically served here between 9:00 and 10:00 PM. The Buckingham pattern of Noritake china (pictured here) was selected by Priscilla and Elvis at the time of their marriage. The original china is in California with Priscilla and Lisa. The flatware on the table is original. The chandelier over the table and the one in the foyer are two of three purchased by Elvis in 1974.
Inset Right: This cabinet on the west wall contains some of the Presley household silver.

Life at Graceland

The Kitchen

As in most homes, Graceland's kitchen swirled with activity. The cooks rarely prepared anything too fancy, though, because Elvis liked the same downhome Southern cooking that he and the people around him grew up on. Elvis, always appreciative of those who worked for him, would sometimes surprise one of the household staff with keys to a new Cadillac. Occasionally, craziness erupted among the pots and pans. Once when Elvis and the guys were playing with fireworks, a whistling chaser landed smack in the middle of a cake, and exploded.

Elvis redecorated and remodeled the kitchen several times. Today, it remains as Elvis last decorated it in the mid-1970's, with all the authentic appliances, dishes and utensils. Its overall look, with harvest gold and avocado-colored appliances, reflects classic 1970's American home fashion. In the spring of 1995, Graceland opened the kitchen to the public. It had remained off the tour because Elvis' Aunt Delta still lived at Graceland and regularly used the kitchen until she passed away in 1993. She had come to Graceland at Elvis' invitation when she was widowed in 1967.

Life at Graceland 21

The TV Room and Pool Room

Lower Left: Descending into Graceland's basement you encounter this completely mirrored staircase.

Top Left: This bar/soda fountain is just inside the door of the TV room. Both the TV room and pool room went from very basic looking recreation rooms to a richly appointed seventies hip, when Elvis and his girlfriend Linda Thompson had the basement rooms redecorated in 1974, by Memphis interior designer Bill Eubanks.

Above: The overall design of the TV room is in perfect step for the taste of the seventies - sectional sofa, chrome accessories, mirrored ceiling and fireplace, "super-graphics" paint job, and all. The lightning bolt on the west wall is part of Elvis' personal logo - a TCB and lightning bolt symbolizing "taking care of business in a flash". Left over from the sixties is the set-up for three built-in televisions Elvis put in after learning that President Lyndon Johnson liked to watch all three major network news shows at the same time. Elvis himself was indeed one to keep up with current news, but he also especially liked to watch college and professional football games, and enjoyed laughing through episodes of comedies and variety shows like "Carol Burnett", "I Love Lucy", and "Dick Van Dyke". Above the TV's is a movie projection screen for home movies and films. For feature film viewing, he tended to rent out a local theater from himself and friends. Among his many favorites were "Patton", the "Pink Panther" films starring Peter Sellers, and the uproarious comedies by England's Monty Python troupe.

Inset Left: The home jukebox built into the television wall has a capacity of 100 singles and is wired for sound all over the house. Much of Elvis' personal record collection is with the stereo in this room. It covers pop, rock, and country, but is mostly gospel and rhythm & blues.

Left: In the corner, three Louis XV style chairs in red leather, a brass-over-wood campaign trunk on an Oriental stand, nostalgic art prints, and various bric-a-brac appoint the pool room.

Right: This pool table long predates Elvis' 1974 redecoration, and has been the key fixture in this room for many years. The tear in the felt top occurred sometime in the mid-to-late seventies when a friend tried a trick shot that did not quite work out.

Below: The distinctive pool room saw a lot of action over the years. Elvis' favorite games were "8-ball" and "rotation", and he wasn't at all shy about moving a ball to his advantage once in a while, playfully testing his friends' courage to challenge him on it. The 350-400 yards of cotton fabric took the decorating crew about ten days to cut, piece, pleat, and hang. Eclectic decorating, now popular again, was an "in thing" in the seventies, and the pool room mixes European, Asian, and American styles of various eras.

Life at Graceland **23**

24 *Elvis Presley's Graceland*

The Jungle Room

Left: Affectionately dubbed the "jungle room" by today's Graceland tour staff, Elvis added this den to the house in the mid-sixties. Even with its custom stone waterfall, it was a fairly typical looking American family room until, one day in the mid-seventies, Elvis walked into a Memphis store named Donald's and in thirty minutes picked out all of this fake-fur-upholstered furniture with its carved wood frames and coordinating tables. Besides the fact that this type of furniture was a wild fad of the time, it also reminded Elvis of Hawaii, a place where he made several movies, gave some important concerts, and vacationed.

Inset left: Elvis often enjoyed his breakfast at this hardwood coffee table.
Inset below: The red and green phones are the original instruments used by Elvis. The green one is a regular phone with multiple lines, and the red one is part of Elvis' intercom system for the mansion.
Above: The green shag carpeted ceiling was trendy in the mid-seventies. Elvis later realized that the carpeting's sound absorption made the room suitable for jam sessions and recording. Elvis had RCA bring in portable recording equipment, park their trucks out back, and run cables into the room for some recording sessions in 1976. In this very room, Elvis, his band, and back-up singers jammed and recorded all of the album "From Elvis Presley Boulevard, Memphis, Tennessee", released that same year, plus six songs for his very last album, "Moody Blue", released in 1977.

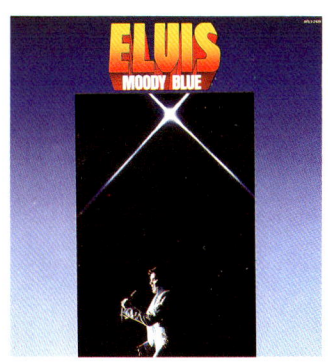

Life at Graceland

Vernon Presley's Office

Above: Elvis' father, Vernon Presley, along with his secretarial staff, handled Elvis' private business affairs, fan mail, correspondence and daily household management from this modest office behind the mansion.
Left: Vernon Presley's own desk, used from the fifties until his passing on June 26, 1979 at the age of 63. Vernon was known to be tight with a dollar, and few of the key furnishings in this room changed through the years.

Below: The office was a popular place to "hang out" during the day at Graceland for various staff and members of Elvis' entourage. This sign on the door clearly states how Vernon felt about it! Vernon had his niece and secretary, Patsy Presley Gambill, hand letter it for him.

PLEASE READ AND OBSERVE
NO LOAFING IN OFFICE STRICTLY FOR EMPLOYEES ONLY! IF YOU HAVE BUSINESS HERE, PLEASE TAKE CARE OF IT AND LEAVE.
VERNON PRESLEY

The Back Yard

These bullets and casings were swept from the floor and dug out of the woodwork of this room. They remain from the brief period in the sixties when Elvis and the guys used this room as a firing range.

Above: For a brief time in the mid-sixties, Elvis and his entourage used a storage room off the office as a backdrop for target shooting, setting up an ammunition table in the back yard and shooting through the doorway into this room.
Above Inset: Remaining shells and bullet casings from the storage room's short stint as a target range.
Right: Outside the office is a swing set enjoyed in the mid-to-late seventies by Elvis' daughter Lisa and her cousins and playmates.

Life at Graceland 27

Back of the House and Pasture

Opposite: The back yard was a tranquil place, with a menagerie of animals roaming the pasture and grounds. Elvis' animal collection included horses, donkeys, dogs, peacocks, guinea hens and a chimpanzee, among others. Elvis donated the peacocks to the Memphis Zoo when one of them put a scratch in his shiny Rolls Royce while admiring its own reflection. Occasionally, the peace was broken when Elvis and his friends held target practice or indulged in one of their notorious fireworks fights, when they playfully shot each other with the multi-colored combustibles. Typically, these backyard battles involved hundreds of dollars worth of fireworks, which were evenly distributed between two competing teams. For protection, the combatants wore goggles, gloves and jackets, while the women watched from the den windows. Twice they came close to setting the house ablaze and once an errant bottle rocket hit a stash of fireworks, which erupted in a rainbow spray of sparks.

Opposite Left and Far Right: The pasture held Elvis' beloved stable of horses. Until the mid-1960s, Elvis' horseback riding was mainly limited to movie scenes, but that changed in 1966 when he presented Priscilla with a horse as a surprise gift. Her enthusiasm was contagious, and he bought himself a golden palomino quarter horse he named Rising Sun. For a time, he called his barn "House of Rising Sun". Elvis soon purchased horses for his entire entourage and their wives, and together they'd gallop, often racing wildly, throughout the pasture. Sometimes, while riding Rising Sun or Bear, his Tennessee Walking Horse, Elvis would trot to the gate or front wall to greet fans and sign autographs. At one point, Elvis transferred his horses to a 163-acre swath of Mississippi land he named the Flying Circle G Ranch. He sold it after a few enjoyable years and returned the horses to Graceland. Horses proved a pleasant diversion for Elvis during the frustrating, final years of his film career, just before his triumphant return in the late 1960s to live concert performances. At the end of Elvis' life, four horses and a pony remained at Graceland. Bear had died in the early 1970s, while Rising Sun passed away in 1986. Today, two members of Elvis' original stable still gallop the Graceland pastures: Ebony's Double, a Tennessee Walker bought in 1975, and Mare Ingram, a grade mare purchased in the 1960s. The golden palomino now at Graceland is a distant relative to Rising Sun. It was brought here by the current staff, who believe there always should be a golden palomino at Graceland. Its name is Sun's Reflection.

The Hall of Gold

Right: The hall of gold is an 80-foot long room in Elvis' trophy building lined with his gold and platinum albums and singles, representing the sale of over one billion records worldwide, more than any other entertainer in the history of recorded voice. From his 23-year recording career, Elvis had 149 songs listed on Billboard's Hot 100 pop singles chart. Of those, 114 made it into the top forty; 40 hit the top ten; and 18 made it all the way to number one. These are just the pop chart achievements. Elvis practically had separate careers in country, R&B and gospel!

Opposite Inset Left: This display case shows some of the trophies Elvis received during his career. The six matching figurines are awards from Cashbox Magazine for some of his top records; the tall trophy with the map of Africa commemorates ten "million sellers" in South Africa from 1956 to 1960; the one that resembles the American Oscar is the "Everybody's Award" from an Australian magazine. Others include a trophy representing a big hit with "It's Now or Never" in Japan; a European award declaring Elvis "favorite world singer"; and a Las Vegas "Entertainer of the Year" award.

Opposite Inset Center: Elvis was nominated for fourteen Grammy awards by the National Academy of Recording Arts & Sciences (NARAS). He won three — the Grammy awards displayed here for "How Great Thou Art" (1967); for the gospel album "He Touched Me" (1972); and for a live concert performance of "How Great Thou Art" (1974). Included in the Grammy showcase is an ebony-and-gold plaque the Academy presented to Elvis. At that time, the award was known as the Bing Crosby Award, named for its first recipient. Now, it is known as the NARAS Lifetime Achievement Award. Other honorees include Frank Sinatra, Irving Berlin, Chuck Berry, Ella Fitzgerald, Mahalia Jackson, Louis Armstrong, Leonard Bernstein, and Paul McCartney. Elvis was 36 years old when he received this prestigious honor.

Opposite Inset Right: Off stage in Las Vegas, Elvis receives his Lifetime Achievement Award from NARAS officials and family of Bing Crosby.

Inset Above: This diamond-shaped plaque was presented to Elvis by RCA Records, along with numerous other awards, on February 25, 1961 at a luncheon in his honor in Memphis. It commemorates his first 75 million records sold.

Inset Below: In March 1960, Elvis took delivery of this console television and stereo on the front porch of Graceland. It was an award from RCA recognizing the sales of 50 million records in just over four years of recording with RCA Records. It is among the awards displayed in Elvis' trophy building.

Elvis Presley's Graceland

32 *Elvis Presley's Graceland*

Elvis' Gen[erosity]

Far Left: After a pair of benefit shows for Memphis-area charities in 1961, Elvis made it an annual tradition to distribute checks to fifty or more of these organizations. In the early sixties, the City of Memphis presented him with this massive plaque as a token of appreciation. His reputation for generosity is fairly well-known. All have heard stories about the cars and jewelry Elvis gave away and the benefit concerts he performed, but very little gets mentioned about the families he supported, the cash he gave away to friends as well as strangers, the homes he bought, the hospital bills he paid - so much of it done privately, quietly, with no public recognition. Perhaps once his dreams of material wealth had come true, it was a special joy to see dreams come true, or hardships disappear, for others. He never forgot what it was like to do without.

Left: On March 25, 1961 at Bloch Arena in Hawaii, Elvis performed a benefit concert raising over $65,000 toward the building of the U.S.S. Arizona Memorial, a World War II monument that had not been completed due to years of stalled fund-raising efforts. Elvis' concert provided the largest single donation to the project and, more importantly, stirred a level of public and media attention that made the completion of the monument possible within a year after his concert. It was a source of quiet personal satisfaction and pride for him and Elvis visited the monument several times over the years. The U.S. Navy placed a wreath there in his honor upon hearing the news of his death in 1977. For some reason, his contribution to this deeply meaningful monument is not widely known today.

Top Left: Elvis purchased former U.S. President Franklin Delano Roosevelt's yacht "Potomac" for $55,000 in January 1964. Pictured here on February 13, Elvis presents the yacht to actor Danny Thomas as a gift to St. Jude Children's Research Hospital in Memphis for them to use for fund-raising purposes. The ceremony took place in Long Beach, California.

Life at Graceland 33

Elvis' Singles
IN THE TOP 20 ON BILLBOARD'S POP CHARTS

Song Title/Year	Pop Chart Peak Position
Heartbreak Hotel (1956)	1
I Was The One (1956)	19
Blue Suede Shoes (1956)	20
I Want You, I Need You, I Love You (1956)	1
Don't Be Cruel (1956)	1
Hound Dog (1956)	1
Love Me Tender (1956)	1
Anyway You Want Me (That's How I Will Be) (1956)	20
When My Blue Moon Turns to Gold Again (1956)	19
Love Me (1957)	2
Too Much (1957)	1
All Shook Up (1957)	1
(Let Me Be Your) Teddy Bear (1957)	1
Loving You (1957)	1
Jailhouse Rock (1957)	1
Treat Me Nice (1957)	18
Don't (1958)	1
I Beg of You (1958)	8
Wear My Ring Around Your Neck (1958)	2
Doncha' Think It's Time (1958)	15
Hard Headed Woman (1958)	1
One Night (1958)	4
I Got Stung (1958)	8
(Now and Then There's) A Fool Such As I (1959)	2
Need Your Love Tonight (1959)	4
A Big Hunk O' Love (1959)	1
My Wish Came True (1959)	12
Stuck On You (1960)	1
Fame and Fortune (1960)	17
It's Now or Never (1960)	1
Are You Lonesome Tonight? (1960)	1
I Gotta Know (1960)	20
Surrender (1961)	1

Song Title/Year	Pop Chart Peak Position
Flaming Star (1961)	14
I Feel So Bad (1961)	5
Little Sister (1961)	5
(Marie's the Name of) His Latest Flame (1961)	4
Can't Help Falling in Love (1962)	2
Good Luck Charm (1962)	1
Follow That Dream (1962)	15
She's Not You (1962)	5
Return to Sender (1962)	2
One Broken Heart For Sale (1963)	11
(You're the) Devil in Disguise (1963)	3
Bossa Nova Baby (1963)	8
Kissin' Cousins (1964)	12
Such a Night (1964)	16
Ask Me (1964)	12
Ain't That Lovin' You, Baby (1964)	16
Crying in the Chapel (1965)	3
(Such an) Easy Question (1965)	11
I'm Yours (1965)	11
Puppet on a String (1965)	14
Love Letters (1969)	19
If I Can Dream (1969)	12
In the Ghetto (1969)	3
Suspicious Minds (1969)	1
Don't Cry, Daddy (1970)	6
Kentucky Rain (1970)	16
The Wonder of You (1970)	9
You Don't Have to Say You Love Me (1970)	11
Burning Love (1972)	2
Separate Ways (1972)	20
Steamroller Blues/Fool (1973)	17
If You Talk in Your Sleep (1974)	17
Promised Land (1974)	14
My Boy (1975)	20
Way Down (1977)	18

Statistics Source: Joel Whitburn, Record Research, Inc.

Elvis' Albums
IN THE TOP 20 ON BILLBOARD'S POP CHARTS

Album Title/Year	Album Chart Peak Position
Elvis Presley (1956)	1
Elvis (1956)	1
Peace in the Valley {EP} (1957)	3
Loving You (1957)	1
Just For You {EP} (1957)	16
Elvis' Christmas Album (1957)	1
Elvis' Golden Records (1958)	3
King Creole (1958)	2
For LP Fans Only (1959)	19
Elvis is Back! (1960)	2
G.I. Blues (1960)	1
His Hand in Mine (1961)	13
Something for Everybody (1961)	1
Blue Hawaii (1961)	1
Pot Luck (1962)	4
Girls! Girls! Girls! (1962)	3
It Happened At The World's Fair (1963)	4
Elvis' Golden Records, Volume 3 (1963)	3
Fun in Acapulco (1963)	3
Kissin' Cousins (1964)	6
Roustabout (1964)	1
Girl Happy (1965)	8
Elvis for Everyone! (1965)	10
Harum Scarum (1965)	8
Frankie and Johnny (1966)	20
Paradise, Hawaiian Style (1966)	15
Spinout (1966)	18
How Great Thou Art (1967)	18
Elvis' TV Special (1968)	8
From Elvis in Memphis (1969)	13
From Memphis to Vegas, From Vegas to Memphis (1969)	12
On Stage-February 1970 (1970)	13
Elvis Country (1971)	12
Elvis as Recorded at Madison Square Garden (1972)	11
Elvis—Aloha From Hawaii Via Satellite (1973)	1
Moody Blue (1977)	3
Elvis in Concert (1977)	5

Elvis' Movie Career

Above: Elvis starred in his first four films in 1956-58, prior to his army induction. They were wildly successful and are considered among the best of all the films he made.

Top: The largest of the exhibit areas in the trophy building contains specially created display cases recognizing significant events in Elvis' life. Elvis starred in 31 films as an actor, making 27 of them between his return from the army in 1960 through 1969. This case is filled with movie posters, Elvis' own scripts and movie-era guitars, and a boxing robe he wore in "Kid Galahad". Elvis' fifth movie, "G.I. Blues" was his first after his army release. Its soundtrack album went to number one on the Billboard album chart for ten weeks, staying on the chart for a total of 111 weeks, the longest chart listing of any Elvis recording. "Blue Hawaii" was one of Elvis' biggest hit films and its soundtrack album was number one for twenty weeks.

Right: Elvis and Scatter, his pet chimpanzee, on a movie set in the early sixties.

Below: On the set of his first movie, "Love Me Tender", Elvis has fun playing "the star" — shades, cigar and all — for a publicity shot.

36 Elvis Presley's Graceland

The Films of Elvis Presley

TITLE/YEAR OF RELEASE — **STUDIO**

1. LOVE ME TENDER (1956) — Twentieth Century Fox
2. LOVING YOU (1957) — Paramount
3. JAILHOUSE ROCK (1957) — Metro-Goldwyn-Mayer
4. KING CREOLE (1958) — Paramount
5. GI BLUES (1960) — Paramount
6. FLAMING STAR (1960) — Twentieth Century Fox
7. WILD IN THE COUNTRY (1961) — Twentieth Century Fox
8. BLUE HAWAII (1961) — Paramount
9. FOLLOW THAT DREAM (1962) — United Artists
10. KID GALAHAD (1962) — United Artists
11. GIRLS! GIRLS! GIRLS! (1962) — Paramount
12. IT HAPPENED AT THE WORLD'S FAIR (1963) — Metro-Goldwyn-Mayer
13. FUN IN ACAPULCO (1963) — Paramount
14. KISSIN' COUSINS (1964) — Metro-Goldwyn-Mayer
15. VIVA LAS VEGAS (1964) — Metro-Goldwyn-Mayer
16. ROUSTABOUT (1964) — Paramount
17. GIRL HAPPY (1964) — Metro-Goldwyn-Mayer
18. TICKLE ME (1965) — Allied Artists
19. HARUM SCARUM (1965) — Metro-Goldwyn-Mayer
20. PARADISE, HAWAIIAN STYLE (1965) — Paramount
21. FRANKIE AND JOHNNY (1966) — United Artists
22. SPINOUT (1966) — Metro-Goldwyn-Mayer
23. EASY COME, EASY GO (1967) — Paramount
24. DOUBLE TROUBLE (1967) — Metro-Goldwyn-Mayer
25. CLAMBAKE (1967) — United Artists
26. STAY AWAY, JOE (1968) — Metro-Goldwyn-Mayer
27. SPEEDWAY (1968) — Metro-Goldwyn-Mayer
28. LIVE A LITTLE, LOVE A LITTLE (1968) — Metro-Goldwyn-Mayer
29. CHARRO! (1969) — National General
30. THE TROUBLE WITH GIRLS (AND HOW TO GET INTO IT) (1969) — Metro-Goldwyn-Mayer
31. CHANGE OF HABIT (1969) — Universal

Theatrically-released concert documentary films:

32. ELVIS, THAT'S THE WAY IT IS (1970) — Metro-Goldwyn-Mayer
33. ELVIS ON TOUR (1972) — Metro-Goldwyn-Mayer

Elvis and Priscilla

Elvis Aaron Presley and Priscilla Ann Beaulieu were married in a private ceremony in front of a few close family members and friends on May 1, 1967 at 9:30 AM in a private suite at the Aladdin Hotel in Las Vegas. A press conference and breakfast reception followed. The couple honeymooned for a few days in Palm Springs, California before returning to Memphis. On May 29, 1967, they donned their wedding clothes again and had a second wedding reception in the trophy room at Graceland to accommodate family and friends who were not able to attend the ceremony in Las Vegas.

Nine months to the day after their wedding, on February 1, 1968 at 5:01 PM Priscilla gave birth to their daughter, Lisa Marie Presley, at Baptist Memorial Hospital in Memphis.

Priscilla is the daughter of Ann Beaulieu and Air Force Captain Joseph Beaulieu, who today is a retired colonel. Captain Beaulieu was stationed in West Germany at the same time as Elvis. Priscilla was introduced to Elvis through a mutual friend in the fall of 1959 during his army stint in West Germany. They formed an instant and lasting bond. Elvis left for home and was discharged from the army in March 1960. The two kept in close touch and Elvis, persistent but always the gentleman, finally wore down the Beaulieus until two years later Priscilla was allowed to visit Elvis at his home in Los Angeles. Her first visit to Graceland was for the Christmas holidays of 1962. She moved to Graceland in early 1963 and finished high school at Immaculate Conception in Memphis that spring.

Elvis and Priscilla were divorced in October 1973. Though Priscilla retained custody of Lisa Marie, there was no formal schedule of visitation, and Elvis and his daughter spent time together regularly. Elvis and Priscilla remained close friends until his death in August 1977.

Today, Priscilla continues to make her home in Los Angeles and is an actress, business woman and mother. She and Marco Garibaldi have a son, Navarone, born in 1987. Lisa Marie, from her marriage to Danny Keough, has a daughter, Danielle, born in 1989, and a son, Benjamin, born in 1992.

Lisa Marie was married to singer Michael Jackson, 1994-96. Lisa's primary focus is on family life, charitable efforts and various professional pursuits.

The 1968 Television Special

The sixties had brought about great change in music and pop culture, great change that Elvis had helped pave the way for over a decade earlier. But, Elvis had become less and less a part of the current pop cultural scene. He had been making one movie after another through the sixties, and much of his music was for movie soundtracks. The films and film-related records had been wonderfully successful, but as the sixties wore on, these films and records, though still profitable, were not nearly so successful as they had been. The public was growing weary of the "Presley formula". The weariest of all was Elvis himself, who had reached a supreme level of frustration and unhappiness with the state of his career. He had hoped to become a serious actor, but Hollywood had other ideas, and Elvis had gone along with them.

It was the summer of 1968. Elvis had last appeared in front of a live audience seven years earlier when he did a benefit show for the building of the U.S.S. Arizona Memorial. In June 1968, Elvis taped a television special called "Elvis" to be aired on NBC-TV in December. The show featured Elvis jamming informally and reminiscing with former bandmates Scotty Moore and D.J. Fontana, and several longtime friends. In other sequences, Elvis takes the stage alone to perform many of his greatest rock & rollers and ballads. He also introduces new songs that would become classics, such as "Memories". There's also a gospel production number. Another production number, paralleling Elvis' own career, traces a young man's journey from a struggling guitar player, through all the challenges, dangers and compromises on the path to his dreams of success and superstardom. Something is lost along the way. Once the dream is achieved, the man realizes that he remains unfulfilled, that he has abandoned his true self, a self to whom he now returns. The '68 Special represents Elvis's own return to his true self.

At the end of the special, Elvis appears alone to sing a brand new song, specially written for the show called "If I Can Dream". The writers had created it based on conversations with Elvis about his own thoughts on what was happening in the turbulent sixties, his feelings about life, and his hopes for mankind. It represents one of the few times Elvis would sing a "message" song, and his passionate performance of it is astounding.

Elvis clearly poured years of pent-up creative energy and passion into this show. His natural talent, charisma, and sensuality had not been diminished by Hollywood or by the passage of time. In fact, Elvis looked, sounded, moved, and grooved better than he ever had. At 33, he was better than anybody in the business.

Left: At the time of this photo, the black leather suit from the '68 TV special was out on loan to the Rock & Roll Hall of Fame. But, still displayed in the trophy building is the burgundy suit from the show's gospel production number.

Elvis in 1969 - 70

Above: This display of costumes, guitars, jewelry, and photographs celebrates Elvis' return to the live concert stage in 1969 and 1970. In January and February 1969, hot from the success of the December 1968 television special, Elvis recorded in Memphis for the first time since 1955, putting in several marathon recording sessions at American Sound Studio resulting in brilliant hits such as "Suspicious Minds", "In the Ghetto", and "Kentucky Rain". On July 31, 1969, Elvis opened at the International Hotel in Las Vegas (re-named the Hilton in 1971) for a four-week, 57-performance engagement that broke Las Vegas concert attendance records. He broke his own record there with another engagement in February 1970 (the slow season in Vegas!), and followed this with a wonderfully successful six-show engagement at the Houston Astrodome. He returned to Vegas in the summer and MGM filmed a critically acclaimed documentary, "Elvis, That's the Way It Is", released to theaters later that year. During the fall of 1970, Elvis took his concert show on the road, his first time to tour in concert since 1957. It was a great time in Elvis' life and career, filled with challenge, excitement and satisfaction.

Inset Above: Elvis delivers his distinctive blend of rock & roll, rhythm & blues, pop, gospel and country music on stage in 1970.

Left: At a press conference Elvis receives a gold Rolex watch from officials at the Houston Astrodome. His six-show engagement there in early 1970 attracted a record-breaking 207,494 people.

40 *Elvis Presley's Graceland*

Elvis' Jewelry

Clockwise From Top Center:

Cross Pendant — A 1973 Christmas gift to Elvis from his girlfriend, Linda Thompson. It is gold, encrusted with small diamonds. In the center are two hearts touching - one made with rubies and one with emeralds, which were Elvis' and Linda's birthstones respectively. He wore the pendant frequently, both on and off stage.

TCB Ring — In the 1970's the initials TCB with a lightning bolt became Elvis' personal logo and that of his entourage. It symbolizes the phrase "Taking Care of Business in a Flash". The famous TCB ring is gold, black onyx, and over 16 carats of diamonds. Elvis wore it extensively, both on and off stage, from the time he had the ring made in 1975.

Gold Award Belt — Presented to Elvis by the International Hotel in Las Vegas in recognition of his breaking all Las Vegas attendance records with his 1969 engagement. He proudly wore it on and off stage for several years.

Gold Rolex Watch — Presented to Elvis by officials of the Houston Astrodome when he played six shows there in early 1970.

Rectangular Pendant — A gift of appreciation from the Kui Lee Cancer Fund. Elvis wore it in the 1973 "Aloha from Hawaii" concert, which benefited this charity. The design is the Hawaiian maile vine in gold and diamonds, with Elvis spelled out in black onyx.

I.D. Bracelet — Elvis gave each member of his entourage an I.D. bracelet like this. It had their first name inscribed on top of the bar, and their nickname within the group inscribed underneath. The guys chipped in to buy this one for Elvis. The bar has the name Elvis on top and the nickname "Crazy" underneath.

Karate Ring — A symbol of Elvis' 8th degree black belt status, given to him by his friend, staff member, and sometime karate instructor, Ed Parker.

"Chai" Pendant — a gold and diamond version of the Hebrew symbol for life. Elvis was raised in the Assembly of God Church, but as an adult, studied many religions and philosophies searching for the truths and wisdom to be found in them all.

Life at Graceland

Elvis' Jaycees Award

Right: This tuxedo on display in the trophy room was worn by Elvis on January 16, 1971 when receiving his award as "One of the Ten Outstanding Young Men of the Nation" for 1970, as named by the Junior Chamber of Commerce (Jaycees). This national award has been given each year since 1938 to individuals who have made great achievements in their particular field of endeavor, illustrating the opportunities available in the free enterprise system. It also recognizes one's service to humanity. The honor visibly moved Elvis and signified acceptance, recognition and respect for his work and for him as a human being-the attainment of his American Dream.

"When I was a child, ladies and gentlemen, I was a dreamer. I read comic books, and I was the hero of the comic book. I saw movies, and I was the hero in the movie. So every dream I ever dreamed has come true a hundred times...I learned very early in life that: 'Without a song, the day would never end; without a song, a man ain't got a friend; without a song, the road would never bend; without a song'. So I keep singing a song. Good night. Thank you."

Transcription from Elvis' acceptance speech. (Elvis quotes from copyrighted music "Without a Song" by Billy Rose.)

Bottom Right: Elvis backstage after receiving his "Ten Outstanding Young Men of the Nation" award, wearing the award medallion and custom tuxedo. **Opposite:** Elvis commissioned **Opposite:** c oil painting in 1969 from the famous artist Ralph Wolfe Cowan. Elvis paid $10,000 for the original portrait and $8,000 for the foreign and US copyrights. As it did in Elvis' lifetime, the original hangs in the trophy building today.

42 Elvis Presley's Graceland

Life at Graceland

Elvis' Guns and Badges

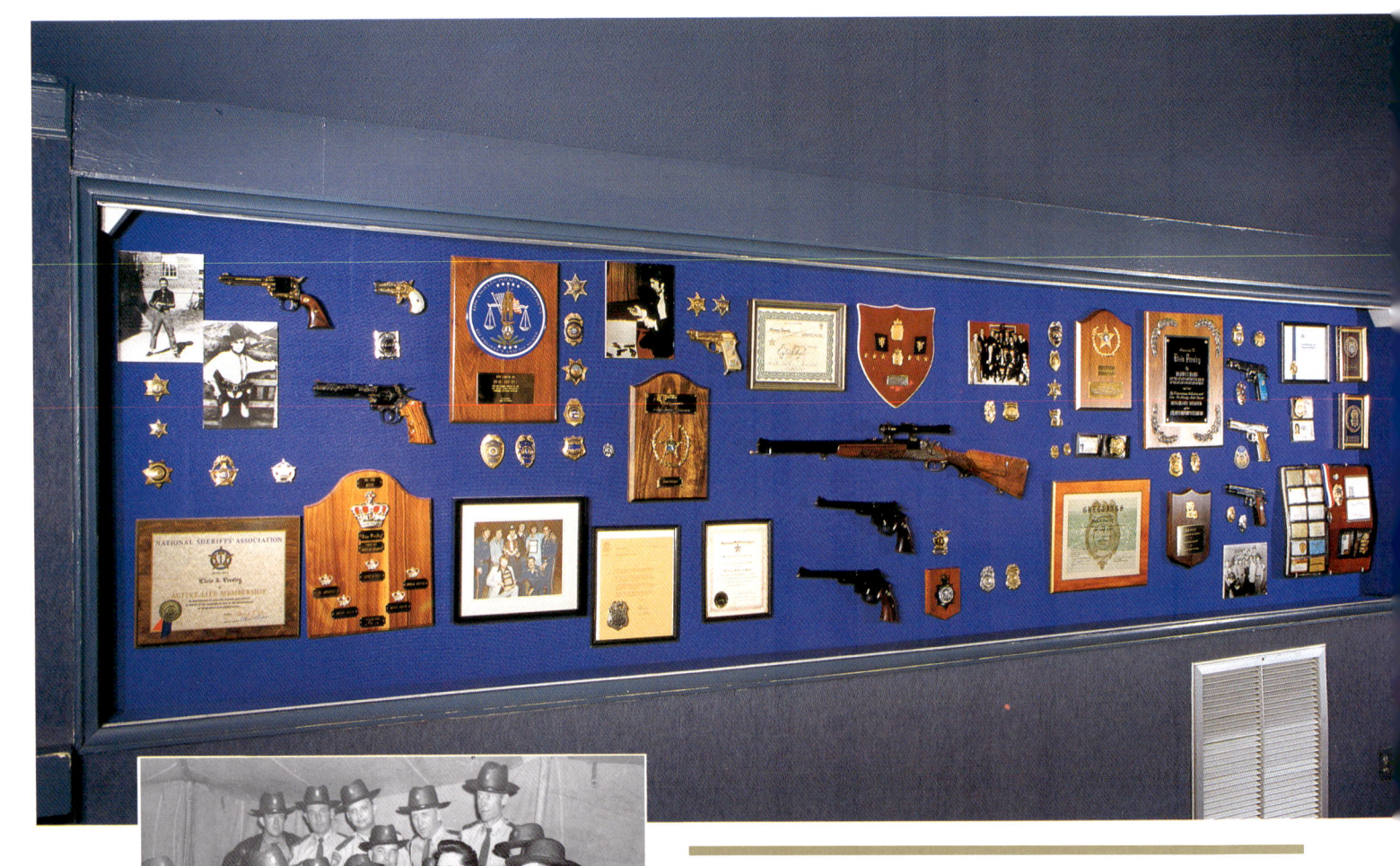

Above: Part of Elvis' sizable collection of guns and badges is displayed in this case in the trophy building, including his gold Pietro Baretta, two Smith & Wesson .357 Magnums, one Python .357 Magnum, one Colt Single Action Frontier Scout .22, one Great Western Arms Derringer, three Colt 45 automatics and a special "over-and-under" 20 gauge shotgun/.22 rifle combination. Like most little boys, Elvis had childhood thoughts of becoming a cop. As a celebrity adult, his public appearances constantly necessitated the presence of police and security people, who made Elvis a member of their fraternal organizations. His interest in collecting badges became well-known and lasted throughout his career. Elvis respected and appreciated law enforcement people and showed interest in their work. They returned this admiration by making him an honorary deputy (sometimes a real one!) in cities and states across the nation.

Inset Left: Mississippi State Troopers pose with Elvis, joined by girlfriend Anita Wood, during his September 1957 return to Tupelo, Mississippi for a special benefit concert. The proceeds contributed to the building of a public recreation center, which continued to receive support from Elvis and still serves the community today.

Citizen Elvis

Left: During his 23-year career Elvis received numerous plaques, proclamations and keys to the city from civic leaders of all levels, and many honors from his fans. The upper case holds some of his civic honors, and the lower case contains items sent to him by his foreign fans.

Below: On December 20, 1970, Elvis met with President Richard Nixon in the Oval Office of the White House. The President of the United States warmly received the King of Rock. Elvis gave Nixon an antique gun, and Nixon gave Elvis a genuine federal narcotics agent badge for his collection.

Life at Graceland

Burning Love: Elvis in 1971 - 72

In 1971, Elvis received his "Ten Outstanding Young Men of the Nation" award, saw the stretch of Highway 51 South running in front of Graceland become Elvis Presley Boulevard, and received the Grammy Lifetime Achievement Award. In 1971-72, his engagements in Las Vegas continued to be standing room only, and his fast-paced concert tours across the nation continued to attract sell-out crowds and critical acclaim. MGM followed his tour in the spring of 1972, filming for "Elvis on Tour", a theatrically released documentary that would win a Golden Globe award for its producers. In June 1972, Elvis was booked into Madison Square Garden, making history with four sold-out shows, attended by fans the likes of John Lennon, George Harrison, Bob Dylan, David Bowie and Art Garfunkel. It was a thrilling time in Elvis' career, but it was also during this time that his marriage to Priscilla was ending. It is said that his poignant recordings of "Always on My Mind" and "Separate Ways" in 1972 reflected some of his emotions following their separation earlier that year. "Burning Love", however, which went to number two on the pop chart in '72, seemed indicative of the state of his career – HOT!

The Dedication of Elvis Presley Boulevard

The City Council of Memphis, Tennessee officially changed the name of Highway 51 South to Elvis Presley Boulevard in June 1971. The first sign was erected in January 1972 at a ceremony outside Graceland with Memphis Mayor Wyeth Chandler and Elvis' father Vernon Presley. When Elvis purchased Graceland in 1957, Highway 51 South and the area known as Whitehaven were "out in the country". By the 1970s, shopping centers, housing developments and apartment complexes had sprung up in the area only 12 miles south of downtown. The actual street address of Graceland is 3764 Elvis Presley Boulevard.

Above: This display case in the trophy building contains costumes, photos and other items from the 1971-72 era. When Elvis opened in Las Vegas in 1969, he asked Bill Belew, the costume designer for his 1968 TV special, to create a completely unique look for him (no boring Vegas lounge singer tux for him!) Elvis was very much into karate at the time, which inspired Bill to create some simple, two-piece, cloth-belted costumes resembling a karate outfit in basic solid colors of black, navy, and white. By 1970, these evolved into one-piece jumpsuits, still relatively simple in design and very trendy for the time (a look other pop and country stars would emulate). With each tour or each Vegas engagement, the suits became more and more elaborate, soon adding metal and rhinestone studding, and matching capes and studded leather belts to the look, and experimenting with various colors. The designs seem dated now, but at that time they were super cool. Bill Belew and his associates designed almost all of Elvis' stage wear and much of his personal wardrobe from 1968 to 1977.

Life at Graceland 47

Elvis: Aloha from Hawaii

Elvis made television and entertainment history with his "Elvis: Aloha from Hawaii, via Satellite" special. It took place at the Honolulu International Center Arena on January 14, 1973. The show was broadcast live at 12:30 AM Hawaiian time, beamed via Globecam Satellite to Australia, South Korea, Japan, Thailand, the Philippines, South Vietnam and other countries. A tape of the show was seen in America on April 4th on NBC attracting 51% of the television viewing audience, and seen in more American households than man's first walk on the moon. In all, it was seen in about 40 countries by approximately 1.5 billion people. Never had one performer held the world's attention in such a way.

Elvis did a complete, untelevised rehearsal show for a packed house on January 12th, then did the actual television special on the 14th. Both shows were a benefit for the Kui Lee Cancer Fund in Hawaii. (Kui Lee was a Hawaiian composer who had died of cancer while still in his thirties.) There was no set ticket price for either performance. Audience members were asked to donate what they could afford. It was projected that the shows would raise $25,000 for the fund, but Elvis proudly announced during the satellite broadcast that $75,000 had been raised.

The soundtrack album "Elvis: Aloha from Hawaii, via Satellite" went to number one on the Billboard pop album chart in 1973, and stayed on the chart at various positions for 52 weeks.

This was probably the pinnacle of Elvis' superstardom. In fact, he redefined the term superstar. Looking back at the footage and photos from this remarkable moment in history, it is hard to believe that Elvis, who was so magnificent in this show, in fine form physically and vocally, would die a little over four-and-a-half years later. After "Aloha" Elvis continued to have successful albums and record-breaking concert appearances all over America, right up until the day he died. But, soon after this show, the decline in his health and personal happiness would become evident. This magical night remains a monument to Elvis Presley's greatness, and it contributed significantly to securing his status as a legend without equal in the entertainment world.

Insert Left: At the end of "Aloha" Elvis tossed this cape into the audience. Graceland recovered it in 1995, a gift from the estate of collector Andrew M. Kern.
Above: This trophy building display case covers the 1973-1974 era. Included from the "Aloha" special are the American Eagle jumpsuit, the corduroy suit he wore as he arrived by helicopter in the opening sequences, and a crown an audience member gave him. Also displayed are other stage costumes from this era. By 1974, the look evolved from heavy studding to lighter weight, but even flashier, embroidery work, and the capes had been phased out. A popular one of the embroidered costumes was the Tiger design show in this case. Tiger was Elvis' nickname in karate, an interest he developed while in the army. By 1974 he had an eighth degree black belt in the Kenpo and Tae Kwon Do styles of the art. Karate-inspired moves had been a part of his on-stage choreograph since his return to concert performing in 1969, and Elvis is credited with doing much to contribute to the 1970s surge in karate's popularity.
Below: For the 1973 "Aloha" special Elvis asked his designer for a costume that would say "America" to his worldwide audience. The American Eagle jumpsuit, which he is pictured here wearing in the show, was the result.

48 *Elvis Presley's Graceland*

Elvis from 1975 - 77

The costumes and memorabilia displayed in this case in Elvis' trophy room reflect his final years of concert tours and recordings. Sell-out crowds still clamored to see him. In Pontiac, Michigan at the newly opened Silverdome, Elvis set a single performance attendance record of 62,500 people on New Year's Eve, December 31, 1975. The year of 1976 was marked by extensive concert tours, Las Vegas engagements, the famous recording sessions in February and October in Graceland's "Jungle Room", and the break-up of Elvis' four-year relationship with steady girlfriend Linda Thompson late that year. Later that same month, Elvis met Ginger Alden, who would become his steady girlfriend until the end.

Elvis wore a white and gold jumpsuit known as the Aztec Sun (pictured below) extensively during his 1977 concert engagements. Between January and June 1977 alone, Elvis gave 55 shows, despite his increasing health problems and hospitalizations for recurring pneumonia, pleurisy, hepatitis, glaucoma, and prescription drug dependency. In June, during Elvis' last time out on the road, shows in Omaha and Rapid City were filmed in preparation for an upcoming CBS television special "Elvis in Concert". Elvis wore the Aztec suit for the TV special, which aired posthumously October 3, 1977. Elvis also wore this suit when he gave his last concert performance ever, June 26, 1977 at Market Square Arena in Indianapolis, Indiana. In July, Elvis was named Favorite Rock Music Star and Favorite Variety Star by Photoplay Magazine.

The next leg of Elvis' 1977 concert touring schedule was to begin on Wednesday, August 17, in Portland, Maine and conclude ten cities later back in Memphis. At that time, it is said that Elvis had talked about slowing down his touring and seeking out new film projects — movies that he would find challenging and in which he could prove himself as an actor. We will never know exactly what his plans were or what might have been the next exciting chapter in his career and his life at Graceland.

Elvis and His Fans

Elvis' level of respect and appreciation for his fans is considered unique among superstars. His connection with them was without parallel.

Elvis had a rare ability – through records, films, concerts, and simply "being" – to communicate something far greater than just entertainment to his audience. Fans felt as if they knew him personally and that he knew them. Romantic fantasies aside, most fans simply felt that Elvis was just like a member of their family. It is a feeling that, even today, brand new fans sense when they delve into the recordings, videos, books and mementos that document the life and work of the incomparable Elvis Presley.

Below: Trophy room displays contain a small sampling of the hundreds of scrapbooks, plaques and other gifts Elvis received from fans through the years, most of which he kept and stored at Graceland.

Left: An admirer from Australia presents her club scrapbook to Elvis on the set of one of his movies in the 1960's.
Above: Fans embrace Elvis backstage during a concert tour in 1970.
Opposite: Two young girls hug Elvis in 1957.
Overleaf: Elvis and his fans through the years.

50 *Elvis Presley's Graceland*

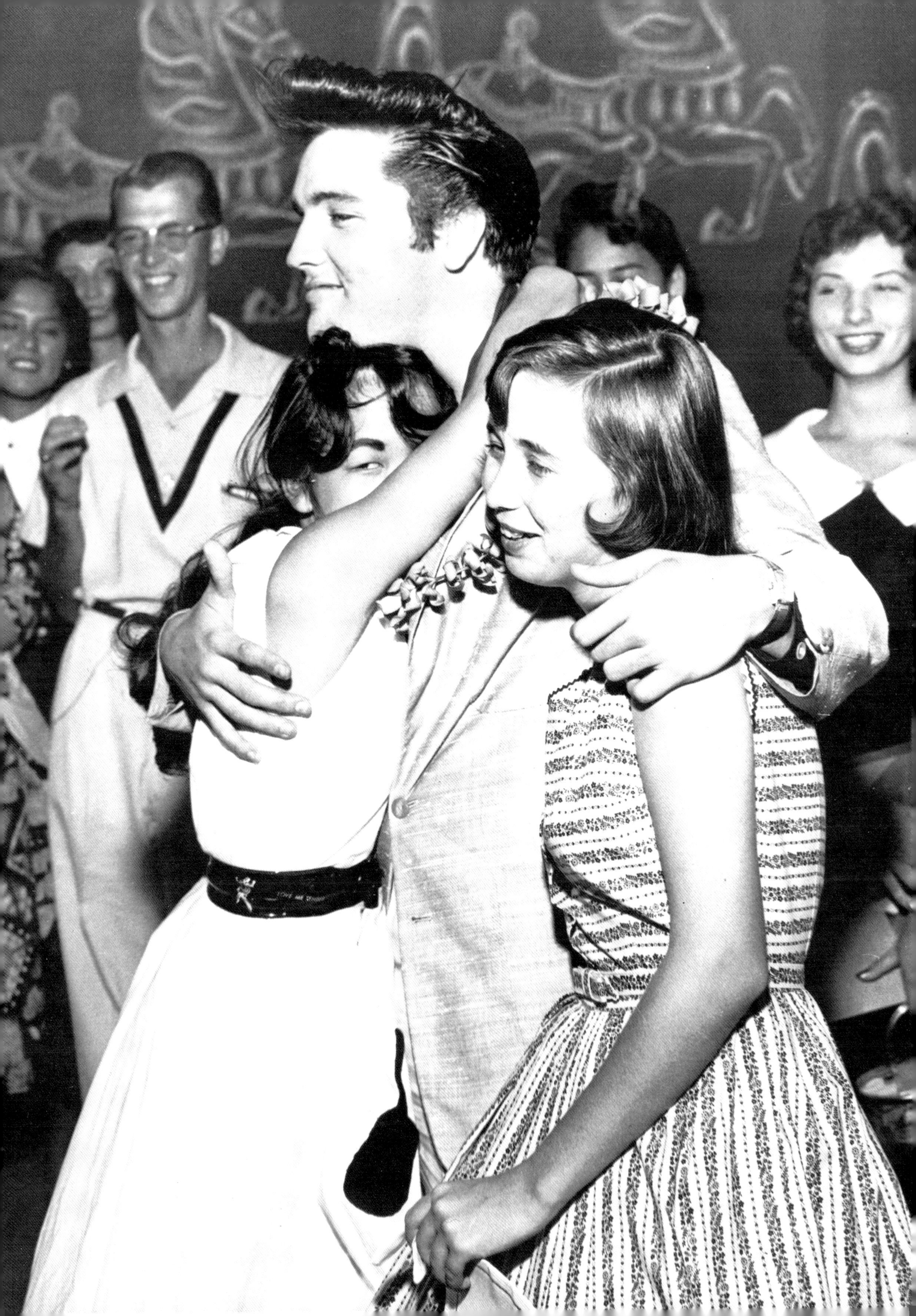

52 *Elvis Presley's Graceland*

Life at Graceland 53

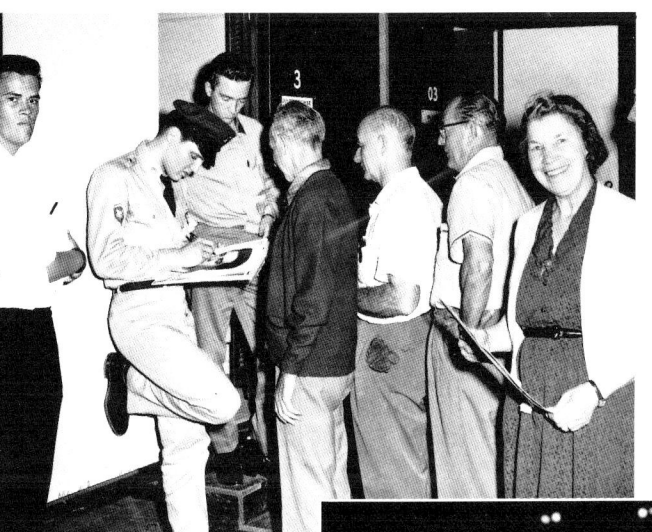

THE PENALTY OF LEADERSHIP

IN EVERY field of human endeavor, he that is first must perpetually live in the white light of publicity. Whether the leadership be vested in a man or in a manufactured product, emulation and envy are ever at work. ⁋ In art, in literature, in music, in industry, the reward and the punishment are always the same. ⁋ The reward is widespread recognition; the punishment, fierce denial and detraction. ⁋ When a man's work becomes a standard for the whole world, it also becomes a target for the shafts of the envious few. If his work be merely mediocre, he will be left severely alone — if he achieve a masterpiece, it will set a million tongues a-wagging. ⁋ Jealousy does not protrude its forked tongue at the artist who produces a commonplace painting. ⁋ Whatsoever you write, or paint, or play, or sing, or build, no one will strive to surpass or to slander you, unless your work be stamped with the seal of genius. ⁋ Long, long after a great work or a good work has been done, those who are disappointed or envious continue to cry out that it cannot be done. ⁋ Spiteful little voices in the domain of art were raised against our own Whistler as a mountebank, long after the big world had acclaimed him its greatest artistic genius. ⁋ Multitudes flocked to Bayreuth to worship at the musical shrine of Wagner, while the little group of those whom he had dethroned and displaced argued angrily that he was no musician at all. ⁋ The little world continued to protest that Fulton could never build a steamboat, while the big world flocked to the river banks to see his boat steam by. ⁋ The leader is assailed because he is a leader, and the effort to equal him is merely added proof of that leadership. ⁋ Failing to equal or to excel, the follower seeks to depreciate and to destroy — but only confirms once more the superiority of that which he strives to supplant. ⁋ There is nothing new in this. It is as old as the world and as old as the human passions — envy, fear, greed, ambition, and the desire to surpass. ⁋ And it all avails nothing. ⁋ If the leader truly leads, he remains — the leader. ⁋ Master-poet, master-painter, master-workman, each in his turn is assailed, and each holds his laurels through the ages. ⁋ That which is good or great makes itself known, no matter how loud the clamor of denial. ⁋ That which deserves to live — lives.

This text, written by Theodore F. MacManus, appeared as an advertisement in the Saturday Evening Post, January 2 in the year 1915. Copyright, Cadillac Motor Car Company.

Elvis Presley's Graceland

Elvis' Continuing Honors and Achievements

Opposite: In 1967, the Cadillac Division of General Motors mailed out scrolls of "The Penalty of Leadership" by Theodore F. MacManus to their customer list. Elvis happened to be in his father's office when the mailing arrived. Elvis liked it so much that he had it framed and hung in his private office upstairs at Graceland. Elvis felt it described his own life and quoted from it often. Now it is displayed in the "Sincerely Elvis" exhibit at Graceland for all to reflect upon.

Below: As long as one is remembered, one is never really gone, so the saying goes. Through Elvis' records, films and over 500 fan clubs, worldwide, the King of Rock & Roll's legend lives on. This corner of his trophy room at Graceland is devoted to the posthumous honors Elvis has received including: induction into the Rock & Roll Hall of Fame; the Award of Merit from the American Music Awards; the W.C. Handy Award from the Blues Foundation; the Golden Hat Award from the Academy of Country Music; and the NARAS Grammy Hall of Fame award for Elvis' 1956 pre-Grammy-era recording of "Hound Dog".

Above: This incredible "Wall of Gold" mounted in the Racquetball Building at Graceland was presented to the Elvis Presley Estate in August 1992, by RCA executives and the Recording Industry Association of America. Elvis had never been awarded all the certified gold and platinum awards he had coming to him during his career, and many he did receive had gone gold or platinum multiple times without receiving certification. Un-awarded record sales also continued after his death. Pouring through old and new sales files, an update audit was done. Presented here is a disc for every Elvis album or single that ever went gold or platinum, one award per album or single, with its highest certified status noted. These 110 different albums and singles, with either gold, platinum or multi-platinum status, made for the largest single presentation of gold and platinum awards in music history. These represent Elvis' sales achievements in America only. (Number 111 was awarded in 1993.)

Inset Right: Centered in front of the wall of gold and platinum records is this nine foot tall multi-paneled, etched glass award recognizing Elvis Presley as the greatest recording artist of all time. It was presented by RCA to the Estate along with the record awards in August 1992.

Life at Graceland 55

Elvis Presley's Graceland

The Racquetball Building

Left: In 1975, Elvis built a 2,200 square foot, two-story structure at Graceland to accommodate his new interest for the sport of racquetball. The building features a bi-level lounge area (pictured here) and one hardwood, glass enclosed racquetball court on the ground floor, and upstairs, Elvis' private dressing room, Jacuzzi spa, and facilities for guests. Elvis was in this building just hours before his death on Tuesday, August 16, 1977. He had been out for a late-night dental appointment and came home shortly after midnight. Elvis, his girlfriend Ginger Alden, along with his cousin Billy Smith and wife Jo played a few light-hearted games, then relaxed in this lounge around the piano.
Inset: This water fountain is an original racquetball building fixture used by Elvis.
Below: Elvis sat at this upright piano on that last day and played and sang. Two of the tunes were "Unchained Melody" and "Blue Eyes Crying in the Rain". Shortly thereafter, Elvis retired to his private suite upstairs at the mansion around 7:00AM to rest for his evening departure to Portland, Maine; the beginning of the next leg of his concert tour schedule. At midday, he was found collapsed upstairs at Graceland and was taken by ambulance to Baptist Memorial Hospital. Elvis was pronounced dead on arrival due to heart failure. In a matter of moments, the shock registered around the world.

The Meditation Garden

Opposite: Elvis constructed his beautiful Meditation Garden in the mid-1960's as a place of refuge and peace. It consists of a curving brick wall with stained glass windows, shrubs and sidewalks, a centrally located pond with fountain, and is appointed with a semi-circle of Greek inspired columns.
Above Right: This swimming pool was added to Graceland shortly after Elvis purchased the property in 1957. The view towards the Meditation Garden is serene and tranquil even today.
Below Right: Elvis and Priscilla in the newly constructed Meditation Garden in the mid-sixties. Elvis' friend Jerry Schilling and his former wife Sandy are pictured in the background.
Opposite Lower Left: Elvis is not known to have expressed an intention to be buried in the Meditation Garden. But, in October 1977, after Elvis' death on August 16, 1977, his father Vernon had the bodies of Elvis and his mother Gladys moved from nearby Forest Hill Cemetery to Graceland for security reasons. In 1979, Vernon Presley was laid to rest between his wife and son. In 1980, Elvis' paternal grandmother, Minnie Mae Presley was buried to the left of Elvis' grave.

Also in the garden is a small bronze tablet in memory of Elvis' twin brother Jessie Garon Presley who was stillborn and whose grave site is still in Tupelo.
Opposite Lower Right: The IHS (In His Service) marble family monument was originally in the family plot at Forest Hill Cemetery. It was moved here in 1977. Elvis loved his home and the Meditation Garden was a special part of it. It is fitting that this garden has become his final resting place.

58 *Elvis Presley's Graceland*

Life at Graceland 59

"Elvis Presley's death deprives our country of a part of itself. He was unique, irreplaceable...he burst upon the scene with an impact that was unprecedented and will probably never be equaled. His music and his personality, fusing the styles of white country and black rhythm & blues, permanently changed the face of American popular culture. His following was immense. And he was a symbol to people the world over of the vitality, rebelliousness and good humor of this country."

—President Jimmy Carter, from the official White House statement marking Elvis' death on August 16, 1977.

Part 3

Elvis' Legend Lives on at Graceland 1977 –

When he died in 1977, Elvis could have left one of the great fortunes of entertainment history, had he been one to worry about financial planning, rather than freely enjoying and sharing his wealth as he did. Elvis' will appointed his father, Vernon Presley, who had long handled Elvis' personal, non-career business affairs, as executor and trustee. The three beneficiaries were Vernon; Minnie Mae Presley, Elvis' paternal grandmother, and Lisa Marie Presley, Elvis' daughter. The will provided that Vernon Presley could, at his discretion, disperse funds to other family members should they be in need. Vernon Presley died in 1979. Minnie Mae Presley died in 1980. This left Lisa as the sole heir to the estate. Elvis' will stated that Lisa's inheritance was to be held in trust for her until her twenty-fifth birthday, on February 1, 1993.

Vernon Presley's will brought about the appointment of three co-executors/co-trustees to succeed him. They were: the National Bank of Commerce in Memphis, which was the bank Elvis and Vernon had done business with; Joseph Hanks, who had been Elvis and Vernon's accountant for a number of years; and Priscilla Beaulieu Presley, who had divorced Elvis in 1973, but had remained a very close friend and was Lisa's legal guardian.

While the estate Elvis left was by no means insolvent, there was a cash flow problem, especially with Graceland costing over half a million dollars a year in maintenance and taxes. It seemed logical for Priscilla and the executors to open Graceland to the public. In late 1981, they hired Jack Soden, a Kansas City, Missouri investment counselor whom Priscilla had worked with in business matters of her own, to plan and execute the opening of Graceland to the public and oversee the total operation. Graceland opened for tours on June 7, 1982.

In 1983, Graceland took over the shopping center plaza across the street from the mansion. From the time the plaza was built in the sixties, it had been a typical suburban strip shopping center. However, almost overnight after Elvis' death, it became an unsightly blemish of tacky Elvis souvenir shops, which carried mostly bootleg items not licensed by the Presley Estate. Upon assuming management of the shopping center property, Graceland began policing the bootleg activities and started an overall facelift, while continuing to honor the existing leases of the plaza tenants. By 1987, all the leases had expired and Graceland began major renovations to the plaza, which continue to this day. Today, all shops and attractions in what is now known as Graceland Plaza are owned and operated by Graceland.

North of the plaza are Graceland visitor parking facilities and the airplanes exhibit, located on an eleven-acre parcel of land Elvis bought in 1962, but had never developed.

Two major developments in the complex across the street from Graceland Mansion were the 1984 return of Elvis' "Lisa Marie" jet and "Hound Dog II" JetStar planes, which opened for tours in a joint venture with the current owners (Elvis' father had sold the jets in 1978); and the 1989 opening of the Elvis Presley Automobile Museum. Continued expansion and enhancement of visitor facilities and the development of new museum projects relating to Elvis and the rock era, incorporating fantastic exhibits and state-of-the-art audiovisuals, are planned for the Graceland Plaza property in the near future.

Graceland is part of Elvis Presley Enterprises, Inc. (EPE), a corporate entity wholly owned by the Elvis Presley Trust. EPE's business extends beyond the Graceland operation in Memphis. It includes worldwide licensing of Elvis-related products and ventures, the development of music, film, video, television and exhibition projects, the management of significant music publishing assets, and more.

Jack Soden's position has evolved to CEO of Elvis Presley Enterprises, and Priscilla Presley is the president. Priscilla and the National Bank of Commerce continue to serve as co-trustees of the Estate. (Joseph Hanks retired from his executor post in 1990.) Lisa Marie stays closely involved with the company management and actively participates in planning and decision making. At the time of her inheritance in 1993, she chose to create a new trust and to keep this management structure intact, including keeping Graceland open to the public for many, many years to come.

Through a monumental body of films, concert videos, recordings, and photographs; through the devotion of thousands of fans in over 500 fan clubs; through the continuing fascination of millions of people all over the world; and within the walls of Graceland, the home he loved, the memory of Elvis Aaron Presley lives on. It always will.

Graceland Plaza

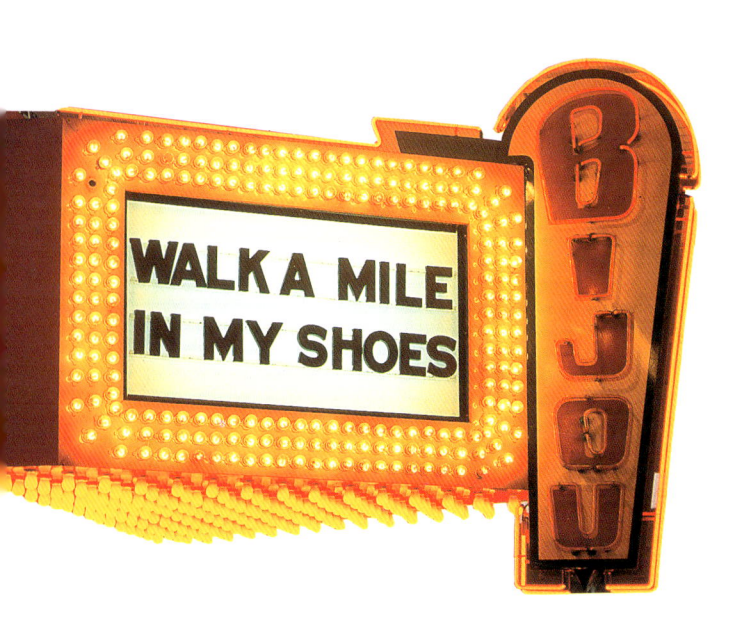

Above: Visitors arrive at Graceland Plaza, an attractive 18-acre complex across the street from the mansion and its 13.8-acre grounds. Here, you may purchase tour tickets, mementos, gifts, and refreshments, and board shuttle buses for the ride across Elvis Presley Boulevard "up the hill" to tour the mansion itself. Attractions available in the plaza are The Elvis Presley Automobile Museum, the intimate "Sincerely Elvis" museum, and Elvis' airplanes.

Above Inset: This official full-service United States Post Office located in the plaza puts a Graceland postmark on cards and letters posted here.

Left: The Bijou Theater features a free screening of the 22-minute film "Walk a Mile in My Shoes" —a fast-paced, yet touching portrait of the life and career of Elvis Presley.

Opposite: Graceland Plaza offers two restaurants: The Chrome Grille serving plate lunches including world famous Memphis barbeque; and Rockabilly's Diner (shown) which features burgers, hotdogs and pizza.

Opposite Top Right: Elvis Threads presents the finest in Elvis-themed apparel and accessories from jackets and t-shirts, to shorts and caps.

Opposite Inset Left: Good Rockin' Tonight provides the best of Elvis in audio, video and print. Bedecked in retro-style neon, you will find an outstanding selection of CD's, cassettes, videos, books and posters.

Elvis Presley's Graceland

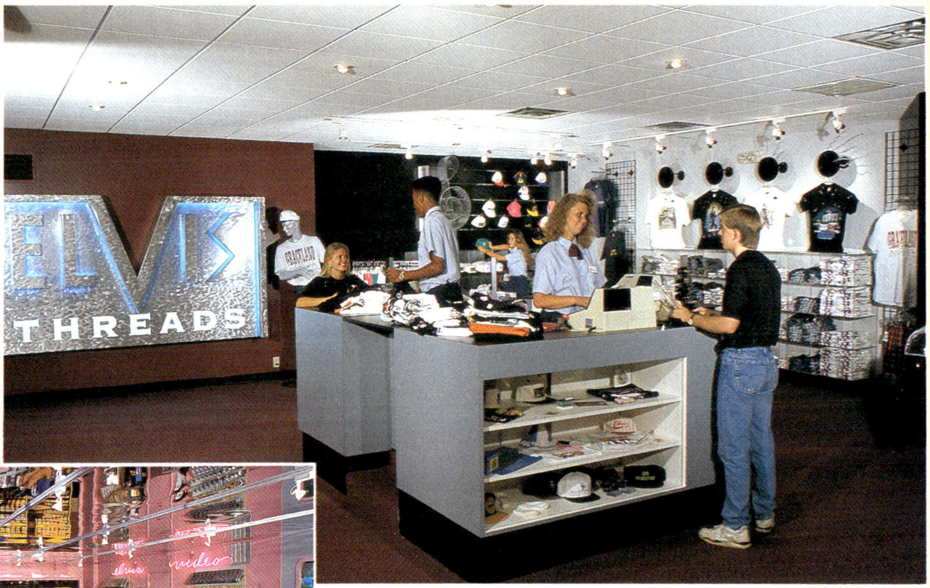
ELVIS
THREADS

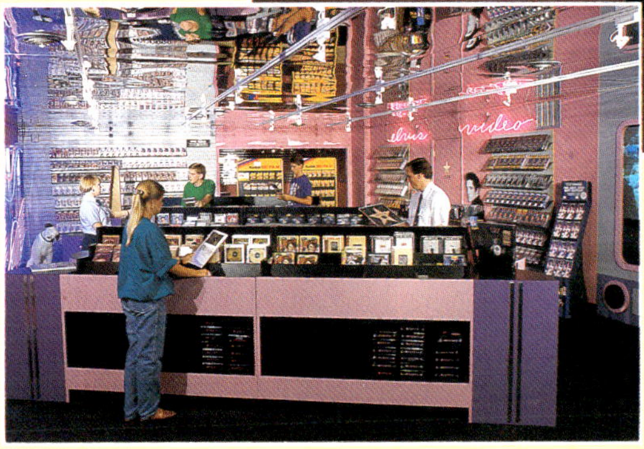

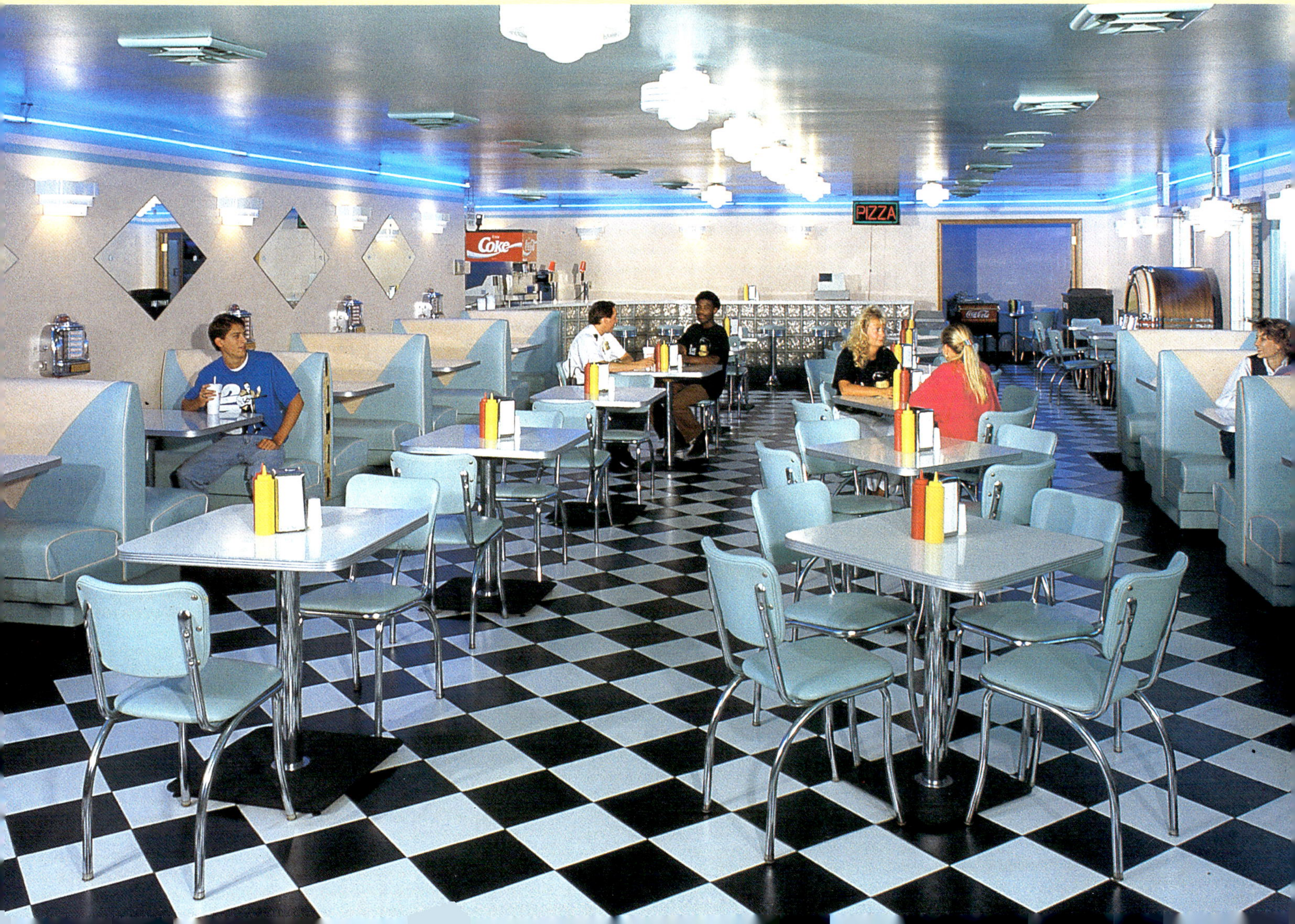
Coke
PIZZA

It is like no other car museum you have ever seen! This 13,000 square foot building houses a landscaped, curbed, carpeted, "highway" leading you past colorful exhibits of vehicles owned and enjoyed by Elvis himself. Along with the 20 or more vehicles, the museum also contains display cases featuring Elvis' driver's license, gasoline credit cards, car registrations, bills of sale, and leather motorcycling attire.

Center: Elvis' 1956 purple Cadillac convertible. Originally, the car was white, but legend has it that when Elvis decided to have it painted purple, he squashed a handful of grapes on it and said "I want it that color".
Above Right: Elvis loved motorcycles and owned many through the years. Shown here are his 1966 Harley chopper, 1965 Honda and two 1976 Harley Davidson Electra-Glide 1200 bikes, along with a couple of his black leather Harley jackets and other gear.
Above Left: Elvis bought this pink Willys jeep in 1960. His security staff used it to patrol the Graceland grounds for a number of years, often giving fans who gathered at the mansion gates a ride.
Opposite Inset Left: Elvis' 1975 Dino Ferrari 308 GT4 Coupe.
Opposite Right: In the auto museum is this "drive-in" theater, where you sit in authentic 1957 Chevy seats and watch a short Elvis video, with sound provided by vintage drive-in speaker boxes.
Opposite Lower Right: Elvis favored this 1973 Stutz Blackhawk during the last years of his life. It features red leather interior and gold-plated trim throughout. When Elvis drove home through the gates of Graceland for the last time on August 16, 1977, he was at the wheel of this fine automobile.

64 *Elvis Presley's Graceland*

The Automobile Museum

Above: Some of Elvis' favorite moto-toys: a go-cart, a dune buggy, three three-wheeled super cycles, a pedal car, one of his fleet of golf carts, and one of his fleet of grass-converted snowmobiles.

Above Inset: Elvis' 1955 pink Cadillac was his mother's favorite, and is almost certainly the most famous car in the world. It has become a universal symbol of 1950's youth culture and rock & roll.

Left: Elvis' 1956 Continental Mark II. It is a collector's item on its own merit, and priceless because of who owned it.

66 Elvis Presley's Graceland

Elvis' Airplanes

Above: Elvis purchased this Convair 880 plane on April 18, 1975 for about $250,000. It was manufactured in 1958 by General Dynamics in San Diego and formerly served as a commercial airline seating 96 passengers. Elvis spent about $750,000 having the jet customized to his specifications and renamed it the "Lisa Marie" after his daughter. His personal logo, the initials TCB and a lightning bold ("Taking Care of Business in a Flash") is painted on the tail. Elvis sometimes called the plane "Hound Dog One" or his "Flying Graceland".
Above Inset: Six leather chairs surround this conference table in the center of the "Lisa Marie".
Above Right: The plane's living room features suede sofas, leather-top game tables, televisions, a video tape player, and quadraphonic stereo. The "Lisa Marie" comfortably accommodated 28 passengers.
Top Right: The private bedroom provides a bed complete with FAA-required safety belt, dressed Elvis-style with a gold-plated buckle.
Left: The "Hound Dog Two" is a Lockheed JetStar purchased by Elvis in September 1975 for $899,702. The customized interior (not pictured) has blue carpet, off-white overhead, and seats in lime green and sunshine yellow. The cabin seats ten and includes a galley, bar, private lavatory, three tables and a Sony stereo system.

Elvis used these planes to travel for fun and for his hectic concert schedule of 1975-77.

Elvis' Legend Lives On

Above Left: Located in the middle of Graceland Plaza, the Sincerely Elvis museum provides a deeper look into the private side of Elvis Presley.

Above Right: Elvis enjoyed karate, football, boxing and a variety of sports and hobbies. Some of his original equipment is displayed here, along with trophies he received from amateur and kids' teams he sponsored over the years. Also displayed is a small sampling of many portraits, hand made items and other gifts he received from his fans and kept through the years.

Above: Some of Elvis' saddles and riding gear.

Right: Elvis and his favorite horse, Rising Sun, a golden palomino quarter horse he acquired in the latter half of the sixties.

68 *Elvis Presley's Graceland*

Personal Mementos

Above: A sampling of Elvis' vast personal record collection reflects his love of all kinds of music, gospel in particular, and an appreciation of a wide variety of artists.
Above Right: Elvis' personal wardrobe items.
Above Inset: This display contains furnishings Elvis used in his bedroom at Graceland in the early days and later stored.
Below: A special photo of Elvis, Priscilla and Lisa taken in early 1971.

The Priceless Gift

In 1971, Elvis and a longtime family friend from Tupelo, Janelle McComb, were reminiscing together at Graceland. Elvis recalled the closeness he had had with his mother, the song "Precious Memories" which had been sung at her funeral, the hardships of his family during his growing up, and all the amazing things that had happened in his life since. He spoke of the values he grew up with, which he still believed in, and how fame and money were fleeting and were not really the important things in life. He asked Janelle to write something he could give Lisa Marie for her fourth birthday, which was to be in February of the following year, so that she could know these things, as he said, "because I might not always be around." Janelle asked if he meant he wanted to give her a "priceless gift". Elvis said "That's right, and be sure to sign it 'Daddy'." Elvis, as well as his father and others, often called upon Janelle to put their feelings in verse. Here is Lisa Marie's own copy of "The Priceless Gift", which brought tears to Elvis' eyes when he read it.

The Priceless Gift

Birthdays are always special
as your fourth one comes to you
and I wondered what I'd give you
Just anything wouldn't do.

I thought of childish treasures
To hang upon your wall
Yet nothing seemed appropriate
or none I could recall.

Money seemed so cold and fleeting
Bought treasures go so fast
And I wanted a gift to please you
And one that would also last.

You know you're sort of special
You are really all we've got
You're mama's bit of Heaven
And daddy's tiny tot.

I closed my eyes—the years rolled by
And I slowly found my way
To a shadowed corner in the attic
'Twas a link to my yesterday.

I raised the lid to a frayed old trunk
And there a priceless treasure lay
A tattered apron with strings still tied
And I know I heard her say—

"Son, I'm now just a precious memory
But don't ever forget one thing
I always tried to guide your life
With these worn out apron strings.

They guided a man named Lincoln
As he steered the Ship of State
It's the only gift I left you
That will never go out of date.

Apron strings changed the course of
History as great men felt their tug
They followed sons onto battle fields
Without the slightest shrug.

They guided both Kings and beggers
Through harmony and strife
Son, you surely must have felt their tug
For how God has blessed your life."

I bowed my head and said a prayer
For I knew God had surely touched
A tattered old trunk so tucked away
And an apron that had meant so much.

So Lisa, I give you the "Priceless Gift"
That surpasses all other things
A whole lifetime of love for you
She tied in her apron strings.

Daddy

J. McCOMB 1971

Christmas at Graceland

Christmas at Graceland was always something special. Tradition held that the house and grounds were decorated from early December through Elvis' birthday, January 8th. Elaborately ornamented Christmas trees could be found in the dining room, living room and several other areas of the house. During his first couple of years at Graceland, Elvis decorated the front lawn with a large Santa, sleigh and reindeer. But in the 1960s, he replaced this with a life-size Nativity scene, a row of lit aluminum Christmas trees that lined the front of the house and hundreds of blue lights outlining the winding driveway. He used this set-up the rest of his life.

Elvis' generous nature shined during the holiday season, a time he especially enjoyed. Each year, he lavished family, friends and staff with expensive gifts, and donated unselfishly to a long list of Memphis-area charities.

Choosing a gift for Elvis, the guy with everything, presented a challenge to all. He appreciated presents that related to his hobbies and interests, and especially those representing not a great expense but a special thought.

Humor always thrived among Elvis' inner circle, particularly in the holiday season. Once Elvis overheard members of his entourage speculating about the size of their customary Christmas bonuses. That Christmas Eve, Elvis, never one to pass up the opportunity for a practical joke, handed out the traditional envelopes and mischievously watched jaws drop as dismayed staff members found $5 McDonald's gift certificates instead of their usual generous bonus checks. When everyone realized it was a joke, they all broke out in laughter, especially Elvis.

Today, the Graceland staff continues Elvis' holiday traditions. From the day after Thanksgiving through Elvis' birthday, visitors can enjoy the interior decorations, the original Nativity scene and even the old Santa set-up.

Opposite Left: Since 1982, Graceland has invited fans to make donations to the Memphis Chapter of the National Hemophilia Foundation, which sells poinsettias during their annual fund-raiser. The flowers are then placed throughout Graceland.

Opposite Right: Graceland Plaza gets the full holiday treatment as well.

Elvis' Legend Lives On